This Book Belongs To

DATE: _____   DAY S M T W T F S

My Why

The best way to stay sober is when you have a strong enough "WHY." Why would you like to stop? Who do you want to stop it for? The WHY can simply be FOR YOURSELF because that will also impact everything and everyone you care about. Take a little time to reflect on your WHY here each day and it will make this journey much easier. It's ok to rewrite the same things here everyday, it's good to remind yourself.

_____

_____

_____

_____

Things that Matter

The fear of losing something important to you can outweigh the gratification of your addiction. Here you can write down the people, places and things that really matter to you. If you already know that your habit is causing problems between you and what matters, it's only a matter of time until you no longer matter as much to them. The truth hurts and heals. Be honest.

_____

_____

_____

_____

You Matter

Everyone has a purpose whether they recognize it or not. Maybe we confuse how we matter by the scale in which we impact other peoples lives. In reality the scale of our impact is unseen. When we impact our family, our friends and our environment in a positive way, it will ripple outwardly, creating more positivity. Same goes with negativity. Here you can write how you impacted your own world in a positive way. It can be as simple as telling someone else how they matter to you.

_____

_____

_____

_____

YOUR PERSONAL SPACE TO DO AS YOU PLEASE

My Why

The best way to stay sober is when you have a strong enough "WHY." Why would you like to stop? Who do you want to stop it for? The WHY can simply be FOR YOURSELF because that will also impact everything and everyone you care about. Take a little time to reflect on your WHY here each day and it will make this journey much easier. It's ok to rewrite the same things here everyday, it's good to remind yourself.

_____

_____

_____

_____

Things that Matter

The fear of losing something important to you can outweigh the gratification of your addiction. Here you can write down the people, places and things that really matter to you. If you already know that your habit is causing problems between you and what matters, it's only a matter of time until you no longer matter as much to them. The truth hurts and heals. Be honest.

_____

_____

_____

_____

You Matter

Everyone has a purpose whether they recognize it or not. Maybe we confuse how we matter by the scale in which we impact other peoples lives. In reality the scale of our impact is unseen. When we impact our family, our friends and our environment in a positive way, it will ripple outwardly, creating more positivity. Same goes with negativity. Here you can write how you impacted your own world in a positive way. It can be as simple as telling someone else how they matter to you.

_____

_____

_____

_____

DATE: _____ **DAY** S M T W T F S

My Why

The best way to stay sober is when you have a strong enough "WHY." Why would you like to stop? Who do you want to stop it for? The WHY can simply be FOR YOURSELF because that will also impact everything and everyone you care about. Take a little time to reflect on your WHY here each day and it will make this journey much easier. It's ok to rewrite the same things here everyday, it's good to remind yourself.

_____

_____

_____

_____

Things that Matter

The fear of losing something important to you can outweigh the gratification of your addiction. Here you can write down the people, places and things that really matter to you. If you already know that your habit is causing problems between you and what matters, it's only a matter of time until you no longer matter as much to them. The truth hurts and heals. Be honest.

_____

_____

_____

_____

You Matter

Everyone has a purpose whether they recognize it or not. Maybe we confuse how we matter by the scale in which we impact other peoples lives. In reality the scale of our impact is unseen. When we impact our family, our friends and our environment in a positive way, it will ripple outwardly, creating more positivity. Same goes with negativity. Here you can write how you impacted your own world in a positive way. It can be as simple as telling someone else how they matter to you.

_____

_____

_____

_____

YOUR PERSONAL SPACE TO DO AS YOU PLEASE

DATE: _____

My Why

The best way to stay sober is when you have a strong enough "WHY." Why would you like to stop? Who do you want to stop it for? The WHY can simply be FOR YOURSELF because that will also impact everything and everyone you care about. Take a little time to reflect on your WHY here each day and it will make this journey much easier. It's ok to rewrite the same things here everyday, it's good to remind yourself.

_____

_____

_____

_____

Things that Matter

The fear of losing something important to you can outweigh the gratification of your addiction. Here you can write down the people, places and things that really matter to you. If you already know that your habit is causing problems between you and what matters, it's only a matter of time until you no longer matter as much to them. The truth hurts and heals. Be honest.

_____

_____

_____

_____

You Matter

Everyone has a purpose whether they recognize it or not. Maybe we confuse how we matter by the scale in which we impact other peoples lives. In reality the scale of our impact is unseen. When we impact our family, our friends and our environment in a positive way, it will ripple outwardly, creating more positivity. Same goes with negativity. Here you can write how you impacted your own world in a positive way. It can be as simple as telling someone else how they matter to you.

_____

_____

_____

_____

YOUR PERSONAL SPACE TO DO AS YOU PLEASE

DATE: _____ **DAY** S M T W T F S

My Why

The best way to stay sober is when you have a strong enough "WHY." Why would you like to stop? Who do you want to stop it for? The WHY can simply be FOR YOURSELF because that will also impact everything and everyone you care about. Take a little time to reflect on your WHY here each day and it will make this journey much easier. It's ok to rewrite the same things here everyday, it's good to remind yourself.

_____

_____

_____

_____

Things that Matter

The fear of losing something important to you can outweigh the gratification of your addiction. Here you can write down the people, places and things that really matter to you. If you already know that your habit is causing problems between you and what matters, it's only a matter of time until you no longer matter as much to them. The truth hurts and heals. Be honest.

_____

_____

_____

_____

You Matter

Everyone has a purpose whether they recognize it or not. Maybe we confuse how we matter by the scale in which we impact other peoples lives. In reality the scale of our impact is unseen. When we impact our family, our friends and our environment in a positive way, it will ripple outwardly, creating more positivity. Same goes with negativity. Here you can write how you impacted your own world in a positive way. It can be as simple as telling someone else how they matter to you.

_____

_____

_____

_____

YOUR PERSONAL SPACE TO DO AS YOU PLEASE

DATE: _____ **DAY** S M T W T F S

My Why

The best way to stay sober is when you have a strong enough "WHY." Why would you like to stop? Who do you want to stop it for? The WHY can simply be FOR YOURSELF because that will also impact everything and everyone you care about. Take a little time to reflect on your WHY here each day and it will make this journey much easier. It's ok to rewrite the same things here everyday, it's good to remind yourself.

_____
_____
_____
_____

Things that Matter

The fear of losing something important to you can outweigh the gratification of your addiction. Here you can write down the people, places and things that really matter to you. If you already know that your habit is causing problems between you and what matters, it's only a matter of time until you no longer matter as much to them. The truth hurts and heals. Be honest.

_____
_____
_____
_____

You Matter

Everyone has a purpose whether they recognize it or not. Maybe we confuse how we matter by the scale in which we impact other peoples lives. In reality the scale of our impact is unseen. When we impact our family, our friends and our environment in a positive way, it will ripple outwardly, creating more positivity. Same goes with negativity. Here you can write how you impacted your own world in a positive way. It can be as simple as telling someone else how they matter to you.

_____
_____
_____
_____

YOUR PERSONAL SPACE TO DO AS YOU PLEASE

DATE: _____   **DAY** S M T W T F S

My Why

The best way to stay sober is when you have a strong enough "WHY." Why would you like to stop? Who do you want to stop it for? The WHY can simply be FOR YOURSELF because that will also impact everything and everyone you care about. Take a little time to reflect on your WHY here each day and it will make this journey much easier. It's ok to rewrite the same things here everyday, it's good to remind yourself.

_____

_____

_____

_____

Things that Matter

The fear of losing something important to you can outweigh the gratification of your addiction. Here you can write down the people, places and things that really matter to you. If you already know that your habit is causing problems between you and what matters, it's only a matter of time until you no longer matter as much to them. The truth hurts and heals. Be honest.

_____

_____

_____

_____

You Matter

Everyone has a purpose whether they recognize it or not. Maybe we confuse how we matter by the scale in which we impact other peoples lives. In reality the scale of our impact is unseen. When we impact our family, our friends and our environment in a positive way, it will ripple outwardly, creating more positivity. Same goes with negativity. Here you can write how you impacted your own world in a positive way. It can be as simple as telling someone else how they matter to you.

_____

_____

_____

_____

YOUR PERSONAL SPACE TO DO AS YOU PLEASE

My Why

The best way to stay sober is when you have a strong enough "WHY." Why would you like to stop? Who do you want to stop it for? The WHY can simply be FOR YOURSELF because that will also impact everything and everyone you care about. Take a little time to reflect on your WHY here each day and it will make this journey much easier. It's ok to rewrite the same things here everyday, it's good to remind yourself.

_____

_____

_____

_____

Things that Matter

The fear of losing something important to you can outweigh the gratification of your addiction. Here you can write down the people, places and things that really matter to you. If you already know that your habit is causing problems between you and what matters, it's only a matter of time until you no longer matter as much to them. The truth hurts and heals. Be honest.

_____

_____

_____

_____

You Matter

Everyone has a purpose whether they recognize it or not. Maybe we confuse how we matter by the scale in which we impact other peoples lives. In reality the scale of our impact is unseen. When we impact our family, our friends and our environment in a positive way, it will ripple outwardly, creating more positivity. Same goes with negativity. Here you can write how you impacted your own world in a positive way. It can be as simple as telling someone else how they matter to you.

_____

_____

_____

_____

YOUR PERSONAL SPACE TO DO AS YOU PLEASE

DATE: _____

My Why

The best way to stay sober is when you have a strong enough "WHY." Why would you like to stop? Who do you want to stop it for? The WHY can simply be FOR YOURSELF because that will also impact everything and everyone you care about. Take a little time to reflect on your WHY here each day and it will make this journey much easier. It's ok to rewrite the same things here everyday, it's good to remind yourself.

_____

_____

_____

_____

Things that Matter

The fear of losing something important to you can outweigh the gratification of your addiction. Here you can write down the people, places and things that really matter to you. If you already know that your habit is causing problems between you and what matters, it's only a matter of time until you no longer matter as much to them. The truth hurts and heals. Be honest.

_____

_____

_____

_____

You Matter

Everyone has a purpose whether they recognize it or not. Maybe we confuse how we matter by the scale in which we impact other peoples lives. In reality the scale of our impact is unseen. When we impact our family, our friends and our environment in a positive way, it will ripple outwardly, creating more positivity. Same goes with negativity. Here you can write how you impacted your own world in a positive way. It can be as simple as telling someone else how they matter to you.

_____

_____

_____

_____

YOUR PERSONAL SPACE TO DO AS YOU PLEASE

DATE: _____ DAY S M T W T F S

My Why

The best way to stay sober is when you have a strong enough "WHY." Why would you like to stop? Who do you want to stop it for? The WHY can simply be FOR YOURSELF because that will also impact everything and everyone you care about. Take a little time to reflect on your WHY here each day and it will make this journey much easier. It's ok to rewrite the same things here everyday, it's good to remind yourself.

_____

_____

_____

_____

Things that Matter

The fear of losing something important to you can outweigh the gratification of your addiction. Here you can write down the people, places and things that really matter to you. If you already know that your habit is causing problems between you and what matters, it's only a matter of time until you no longer matter as much to them. The truth hurts and heals. Be honest.

_____

_____

_____

_____

You Matter

Everyone has a purpose whether they recognize it or not. Maybe we confuse how we matter by the scale in which we impact other peoples lives. In reality the scale of our impact is unseen. When we impact our family, our friends and our environment in a positive way, it will ripple outwardly, creating more positivity. Same goes with negativity. Here you can write how you impacted your own world in a positive way. It can be as simple as telling someone else how they matter to you.

_____

_____

_____

_____

YOUR PERSONAL SPACE TO DO AS YOU PLEASE

DATE: _____

My Why

The best way to stay sober is when you have a strong enough "WHY." Why would you like to stop? Who do you want to stop it for? The WHY can simply be FOR YOURSELF because that will also impact everything and everyone you care about. Take a little time to reflect on your WHY here each day and it will make this journey much easier. It's ok to rewrite the same things here everyday, it's good to remind yourself.

_____

_____

_____

_____

Things that Matter

The fear of losing something important to you can outweigh the gratification of your addiction. Here you can write down the people, places and things that really matter to you. If you already know that your habit is causing problems between you and what matters, it's only a matter of time until you no longer matter as much to them. The truth hurts and heals. Be honest.

_____

_____

_____

_____

You Matter

Everyone has a purpose whether they recognize it or not. Maybe we confuse how we matter by the scale in which we impact other peoples lives. In reality the scale of our impact is unseen. When we impact our family, our friends and our environment in a positive way, it will ripple outwardly, creating more positivity. Same goes with negativity. Here you can write how you impacted your own world in a positive way. It can be as simple as telling someone else how they matter to you.

_____

_____

_____

_____

YOUR PERSONAL SPACE TO DO AS YOU PLEASE

DATE: _____

My Why

The best way to stay sober is when you have a strong enough "WHY." Why would you like to stop? Who do you want to stop it for? The WHY can simply be FOR YOURSELF because that will also impact everything and everyone you care about. Take a little time to reflect on your WHY here each day and it will make this journey much easier. It's ok to rewrite the same things here everyday, it's good to remind yourself.

_____

_____

_____

_____

Things that Matter

The fear of losing something important to you can outweigh the gratification of your addiction. Here you can write down the people, places and things that really matter to you. If you already know that your habit is causing problems between you and what matters, it's only a matter of time until you no longer matter as much to them. The truth hurts and heals. Be honest.

_____

_____

_____

_____

You Matter

Everyone has a purpose whether they recognize it or not. Maybe we confuse how we matter by the scale in which we impact other peoples lives. In reality the scale of our impact is unseen. When we impact our family, our friends and our environment in a positive way, it will ripple outwardly, creating more positivity. Same goes with negativity. Here you can write how you impacted your own world in a positive way. It can be as simple as telling someone else how they matter to you.

_____

_____

_____

_____

YOUR PERSONAL SPACE TO DO AS YOU PLEASE

DATE: _____ **DAY** S M T W T F S

My Why

The best way to stay sober is when you have a strong enough "WHY." Why would you like to stop? Who do you want to stop it for? The WHY can simply be FOR YOURSELF because that will also impact everything and everyone you care about. Take a little time to reflect on your WHY here each day and it will make this journey much easier. It's ok to rewrite the same things here everyday, it's good to remind yourself.

_____

_____

_____

_____

Things that Matter

The fear of losing something important to you can outweigh the gratification of your addiction. Here you can write down the people, places and things that really matter to you. If you already know that your habit is causing problems between you and what matters, it's only a matter of time until you no longer matter as much to them. The truth hurts and heals. Be honest.

_____

_____

_____

_____

You Matter

Everyone has a purpose whether they recognize it or not. Maybe we confuse how we matter by the scale in which we impact other peoples lives. In reality the scale of our impact is unseen. When we impact our family, our friends and our environment in a positive way, it will ripple outwardly, creating more positivity. Same goes with negativity. Here you can write how you impacted your own world in a positive way. It can be as simple as telling someone else how they matter to you.

_____

_____

_____

_____

YOUR PERSONAL SPACE TO DO AS YOU PLEASE

My Why

The best way to stay sober is when you have a strong enough "WHY." Why would you like to stop? Who do you want to stop it for? The WHY can simply be FOR YOURSELF because that will also impact everything and everyone you care about. Take a little time to reflect on your WHY here each day and it will make this journey much easier. It's ok to rewrite the same things here everyday, it's good to remind yourself.

_____
_____
_____
_____

Things that Matter

The fear of losing something important to you can outweigh the gratification of your addiction. Here you can write down the people, places and things that really matter to you. If you already know that your habit is causing problems between you and what matters, it's only a matter of time until you no longer matter as much to them. The truth hurts and heals. Be honest.

_____
_____
_____
_____

You Matter

Everyone has a purpose whether they recognize it or not. Maybe we confuse how we matter by the scale in which we impact other peoples lives. In reality the scale of our impact is unseen. When we impact our family, our friends and our environment in a positive way, it will ripple outwardly, creating more positivity. Same goes with negativity. Here you can write how you impacted your own world in a positive way. It can be as simple as telling someone else how they matter to you.

_____
_____
_____
_____

YOUR PERSONAL SPACE TO DO AS YOU PLEASE

My Why

The best way to stay sober is when you have a strong enough "WHY." Why would you like to stop? Who do you want to stop it for? The WHY can simply be FOR YOURSELF because that will also impact everything and everyone you care about. Take a little time to reflect on your WHY here each day and it will make this journey much easier. It's ok to rewrite the same things here everyday, it's good to remind yourself.

_____

_____

_____

Things that Matter

The fear of losing something important to you can outweigh the gratification of your addiction. Here you can write down the people, places and things that really matter to you. If you already know that your habit is causing problems between you and what matters, it's only a matter of time until you no longer matter as much to them. The truth hurts and heals. Be honest.

_____

_____

_____

You Matter

Everyone has a purpose whether they recognize it or not. Maybe we confuse how we matter by the scale in which we impact other peoples lives. In reality the scale of our impact is unseen. When we impact our family, our friends and our environment in a positive way, it will ripple outwardly, creating more positivity. Same goes with negativity. Here you can write how you impacted your own world in a positive way. It can be as simple as telling someone else how they matter to you.

_____

_____

_____

_____

YOUR PERSONAL SPACE TO DO AS YOU PLEASE

My Why

The best way to stay sober is when you have a strong enough "WHY." Why would you like to stop? Who do you want to stop it for? The WHY can simply be FOR YOURSELF because that will also impact everything and everyone you care about. Take a little time to reflect on your WHY here each day and it will make this journey much easier. It's ok to rewrite the same things here everyday, it's good to remind yourself.

_____

_____

_____

_____

Things that Matter

The fear of losing something important to you can outweigh the gratification of your addiction. Here you can write down the people, places and things that really matter to you. If you already know that your habit is causing problems between you and what matters, it's only a matter of time until you no longer matter as much to them. The truth hurts and heals. Be honest.

_____

_____

_____

_____

You Matter

Everyone has a purpose whether they recognize it or not. Maybe we confuse how we matter by the scale in which we impact other peoples lives. In reality the scale of our impact is unseen. When we impact our family, our friends and our environment in a positive way, it will ripple outwardly, creating more positivity. Same goes with negativity. Here you can write how you impacted your own world in a positive way. It can be as simple as telling someone else how they matter to you.

_____

_____

_____

_____

YOUR PERSONAL SPACE TO DO AS YOU PLEASE

DATE: _____ **DAY** S M T W T F S

My Why

The best way to stay sober is when you have a strong enough "WHY." Why would you like to stop? Who do you want to stop it for? The WHY can simply be FOR YOURSELF because that will also impact everything and everyone you care about. Take a little time to reflect on your WHY here each day and it will make this journey much easier. It's ok to rewrite the same things here everyday, it's good to remind yourself.

_____

_____

_____

_____

Things that Matter

The fear of losing something important to you can outweigh the gratification of your addiction. Here you can write down the people, places and things that really matter to you. If you already know that your habit is causing problems between you and what matters, it's only a matter of time until you no longer matter as much to them. The truth hurts and heals. Be honest.

_____

_____

_____

_____

You Matter

Everyone has a purpose whether they recognize it or not. Maybe we confuse how we matter by the scale in which we impact other peoples lives. In reality the scale of our impact is unseen. When we impact our family, our friends and our environment in a positive way, it will ripple outwardly, creating more positivity. Same goes with negativity. Here you can write how you impacted your own world in a positive way. It can be as simple as telling someone else how they matter to you.

_____

_____

_____

_____

YOUR PERSONAL SPACE TO DO AS YOU PLEASE

DATE: _____ **DAY** S M T W T F S

My Why

The best way to stay sober is when you have a strong enough "WHY." Why would you like to stop? Who do you want to stop it for? The WHY can simply be FOR YOURSELF because that will also impact everything and everyone you care about. Take a little time to reflect on your WHY here each day and it will make this journey much easier. It's ok to rewrite the same things here everyday, it's good to remind yourself.

_____

_____

_____

_____

Things that Matter

The fear of losing something important to you can outweigh the gratification of your addiction. Here you can write down the people, places and things that really matter to you. If you already know that your habit is causing problems between you and what matters, it's only a matter of time until you no longer matter as much to them. The truth hurts and heals. Be honest.

_____

_____

_____

_____

You Matter

Everyone has a purpose whether they recognize it or not. Maybe we confuse how we matter by the scale in which we impact other peoples lives. In reality the scale of our impact is unseen. When we impact our family, our friends and our environment in a positive way, it will ripple outwardly, creating more positivity. Same goes with negativity. Here you can write how you impacted your own world in a positive way. It can be as simple as telling someone else how they matter to you.

_____

_____

_____

_____

YOUR PERSONAL SPACE TO DO AS YOU PLEASE

DATE: _____ **DAY** S M T W T F S

My Why

The best way to stay sober is when you have a strong enough "WHY." Why would you like to stop? Who do you want to stop it for? The WHY can simply be FOR YOURSELF because that will also impact everything and everyone you care about. Take a little time to reflect on your WHY here each day and it will make this journey much easier. It's ok to rewrite the same things here everyday, it's good to remind yourself.

_____

_____

_____

Things that Matter

The fear of losing something important to you can outweigh the gratification of your addiction. Here you can write down the people, places and things that really matter to you. If you already know that your habit is causing problems between you and what matters, it's only a matter of time until you no longer matter as much to them. The truth hurts and heals. Be honest.

_____

_____

_____

You Matter

Everyone has a purpose whether they recognize it or not. Maybe we confuse how we matter by the scale in which we impact other peoples lives. In reality the scale of our impact is unseen. When we impact our family, our friends and our environment in a positive way, it will ripple outwardly, creating more positivity. Same goes with negativity. Here you can write how you impacted your own world in a positive way. It can be as simple as telling someone else how they matter to you.

_____

_____

_____

YOUR PERSONAL SPACE TO DO AS YOU PLEASE

DATE: _____ **DAY S M T W T F S**

My Why

The best way to stay sober is when you have a strong enough "WHY." Why would you like to stop? Who do you want to stop it for? The WHY can simply be FOR YOURSELF because that will also impact everything and everyone you care about. Take a little time to reflect on your WHY here each day and it will make this journey much easier. It's ok to rewrite the same things here everyday, it's good to remind yourself.

_____

_____

_____

_____

Things that Matter

The fear of losing something important to you can outweigh the gratification of your addiction. Here you can write down the people, places and things that really matter to you. If you already know that your habit is causing problems between you and what matters, it's only a matter of time until you no longer matter as much to them. The truth hurts and heals. Be honest.

_____

_____

_____

_____

You Matter

Everyone has a purpose whether they recognize it or not. Maybe we confuse how we matter by the scale in which we impact other peoples lives. In reality the scale of our impact is unseen. When we impact our family, our friends and our environment in a positive way, it will ripple outwardly, creating more positivity. Same goes with negativity. Here you can write how you impacted your own world in a positive way. It can be as simple as telling someone else how they matter to you.

_____

_____

_____

_____

YOUR PERSONAL SPACE TO DO AS YOU PLEASE

DATE: _____   **DAY** S M T W T F S

My Why

The best way to stay sober is when you have a strong enough "WHY." Why would you like to stop? Who do you want to stop it for? The WHY can simply be FOR YOURSELF because that will also impact everything and everyone you care about. Take a little time to reflect on your WHY here each day and it will make this journey much easier. It's ok to rewrite the same things here everyday, it's good to remind yourself.

_____

_____

_____

_____

Things that Matter

The fear of losing something important to you can outweigh the gratification of your addiction. Here you can write down the people, places and things that really matter to you. If you already know that your habit is causing problems between you and what matters, it's only a matter of time until you no longer matter as much to them. The truth hurts and heals. Be honest.

_____

_____

_____

_____

You Matter

Everyone has a purpose whether they recognize it or not. Maybe we confuse how we matter by the scale in which we impact other peoples lives. In reality the scale of our impact is unseen. When we impact our family, our friends and our environment in a positive way, it will ripple outwardly, creating more positivity. Same goes with negativity. Here you can write how you impacted your own world in a positive way. It can be as simple as telling someone else how they matter to you.

_____

_____

_____

_____

YOUR PERSONAL SPACE TO DO AS YOU PLEASE

My Why

The best way to stay sober is when you have a strong enough "WHY." Why would you like to stop? Who do you want to stop it for? The WHY can simply be FOR YOURSELF because that will also impact everything and everyone you care about. Take a little time to reflect on your WHY here each day and it will make this journey much easier. It's ok to rewrite the same things here everyday, it's good to remind yourself.

_____

_____

_____

_____

Things that Matter

The fear of losing something important to you can outweigh the gratification of your addiction. Here you can write down the people, places and things that really matter to you. If you already know that your habit is causing problems between you and what matters, it's only a matter of time until you no longer matter as much to them. The truth hurts and heals. Be honest.

_____

_____

_____

_____

You Matter

Everyone has a purpose whether they recognize it or not. Maybe we confuse how we matter by the scale in which we impact other peoples lives. In reality the scale of our impact is unseen. When we impact our family, our friends and our environment in a positive way, it will ripple outwardly, creating more positivity. Same goes with negativity. Here you can write how you impacted your own world in a positive way. It can be as simple as telling someone else how they matter to you.

_____

_____

_____

_____

YOUR PERSONAL SPACE TO DO AS YOU PLEASE

DATE: _____ DAY S M T W T F S

My Why

The best way to stay sober is when you have a strong enough "WHY." Why would you like to stop? Who do you want to stop it for? The WHY can simply be FOR YOURSELF because that will also impact everything and everyone you care about. Take a little time to reflect on your WHY here each day and it will make this journey much easier. It's ok to rewrite the same things here everyday, it's good to remind yourself.

_____

_____

_____

_____

Things that Matter

The fear of losing something important to you can outweigh the gratification of your addiction. Here you can write down the people, places and things that really matter to you. If you already know that your habit is causing problems between you and what matters, it's only a matter of time until you no longer matter as much to them. The truth hurts and heals. Be honest.

_____

_____

_____

_____

You Matter

Everyone has a purpose whether they recognize it or not. Maybe we confuse how we matter by the scale in which we impact other peoples lives. In reality the scale of our impact is unseen. When we impact our family, our friends and our environment in a positive way, it will ripple outwardly, creating more positivity. Same goes with negativity. Here you can write how you impacted your own world in a positive way. It can be as simple as telling someone else how they matter to you.

_____

_____

_____

_____

YOUR PERSONAL SPACE TO DO AS YOU PLEASE

DATE: _____ **DAY** S M T W T F S

My Why

The best way to stay sober is when you have a strong enough "WHY." Why would you like to stop? Who do you want to stop it for? The WHY can simply be FOR YOURSELF because that will also impact everything and everyone you care about. Take a little time to reflect on your WHY here each day and it will make this journey much easier. It's ok to rewrite the same things here everyday, it's good to remind yourself.

_____

_____

_____

Things that Matter

The fear of losing something important to you can outweigh the gratification of your addiction. Here you can write down the people, places and things that really matter to you. If you already know that your habit is causing problems between you and what matters, it's only a matter of time until you no longer matter as much to them. The truth hurts and heals. Be honest.

_____

_____

_____

You Matter

Everyone has a purpose whether they recognize it or not. Maybe we confuse how we matter by the scale in which we impact other peoples lives. In reality the scale of our impact is unseen. When we impact our family, our friends and our environment in a positive way, it will ripple outwardly, creating more positivity. Same goes with negativity. Here you can write how you impacted your own world in a positive way. It can be as simple as telling someone else how they matter to you.

_____

_____

_____

YOUR PERSONAL SPACE TO DO AS YOU PLEASE

My Why

The best way to stay sober is when you have a strong enough "WHY." Why would you like to stop? Who do you want to stop it for? The WHY can simply be FOR YOURSELF because that will also impact everything and everyone you care about. Take a little time to reflect on your WHY here each day and it will make this journey much easier. It's ok to rewrite the same things here everyday, it's good to remind yourself.

_____

_____

_____

Things that Matter

The fear of losing something important to you can outweigh the gratification of your addiction. Here you can write down the people, places and things that really matter to you. If you already know that your habit is causing problems between you and what matters, it's only a matter of time until you no longer matter as much to them. The truth hurts and heals. Be honest.

_____

_____

_____

You Matter

Everyone has a purpose whether they recognize it or not. Maybe we confuse how we matter by the scale in which we impact other peoples lives. In reality the scale of our impact is unseen. When we impact our family, our friends and our environment in a positive way, it will ripple outwardly, creating more positivity. Same goes with negativity. Here you can write how you impacted your own world in a positive way. It can be as simple as telling someone else how they matter to you.

_____

_____

_____

YOUR PERSONAL SPACE TO DO AS YOU PLEASE

My Why

The best way to stay sober is when you have a strong enough "WHY." Why would you like to stop? Who do you want to stop it for? The WHY can simply be FOR YOURSELF because that will also impact everything and everyone you care about. Take a little time to reflect on your WHY here each day and it will make this journey much easier. It's ok to rewrite the same things here everyday, it's good to remind yourself.

_____
_____
_____
_____

Things that Matter

The fear of losing something important to you can outweigh the gratification of your addiction. Here you can write down the people, places and things that really matter to you. If you already know that your habit is causing problems between you and what matters, it's only a matter of time until you no longer matter as much to them. The truth hurts and heals. Be honest.

_____
_____
_____
_____

You Matter

Everyone has a purpose whether they recognize it or not. Maybe we confuse how we matter by the scale in which we impact other peoples lives. In reality the scale of our impact is unseen. When we impact our family, our friends and our environment in a positive way, it will ripple outwardly, creating more positivity. Same goes with negativity. Here you can write how you impacted your own world in a positive way. It can be as simple as telling someone else how they matter to you.

_____
_____
_____
_____

YOUR PERSONAL SPACE TO DO AS YOU PLEASE

DATE: _____ **DAY** S M T W T F S

My Why

The best way to stay sober is when you have a strong enough "WHY." Why would you like to stop? Who do you want to stop it for? The WHY can simply be FOR YOURSELF because that will also impact everything and everyone you care about. Take a little time to reflect on your WHY here each day and it will make this journey much easier. It's ok to rewrite the same things here everyday, it's good to remind yourself.

_____

_____

_____

_____

Things that Matter

The fear of losing something important to you can outweigh the gratification of your addiction. Here you can write down the people, places and things that really matter to you. If you already know that your habit is causing problems between you and what matters, it's only a matter of time until you no longer matter as much to them. The truth hurts and heals. Be honest.

_____

_____

_____

_____

You Matter

Everyone has a purpose whether they recognize it or not. Maybe we confuse how we matter by the scale in which we impact other peoples lives. In reality the scale of our impact is unseen. When we impact our family, our friends and our environment in a positive way, it will ripple outwardly, creating more positivity. Same goes with negativity. Here you can write how you impacted your own world in a positive way. It can be as simple as telling someone else how they matter to you.

_____

_____

_____

_____

YOUR PERSONAL SPACE TO DO AS YOU PLEASE

DATE: _____ **DAY** S M T W T F S

My Why

The best way to stay sober is when you have a strong enough "WHY." Why would you like to stop? Who do you want to stop it for? The WHY can simply be FOR YOURSELF because that will also impact everything and everyone you care about. Take a little time to reflect on your WHY here each day and it will make this journey much easier. It's ok to rewrite the same things here everyday, it's good to remind yourself.

_____

_____

_____

_____

Things that Matter

The fear of losing something important to you can outweigh the gratification of your addiction. Here you can write down the people, places and things that really matter to you. If you already know that your habit is causing problems between you and what matters, it's only a matter of time until you no longer matter as much to them. The truth hurts and heals. Be honest.

_____

_____

_____

_____

You Matter

Everyone has a purpose whether they recognize it or not. Maybe we confuse how we matter by the scale in which we impact other peoples lives. In reality the scale of our impact is unseen. When we impact our family, our friends and our environment in a positive way, it will ripple outwardly, creating more positivity. Same goes with negativity. Here you can write how you impacted your own world in a positive way. It can be as simple as telling someone else how they matter to you.

_____

_____

_____

_____

YOUR PERSONAL SPACE TO DO AS YOU PLEASE

My Why

The best way to stay sober is when you have a strong enough "WHY." Why would you like to stop? Who do you want to stop it for? The WHY can simply be FOR YOURSELF because that will also impact everything and everyone you care about. Take a little time to reflect on your WHY here each day and it will make this journey much easier. It's ok to rewrite the same things here everyday, it's good to remind yourself.

_____

_____

_____

_____

Things that Matter

The fear of losing something important to you can outweigh the gratification of your addiction. Here you can write down the people, places and things that really matter to you. If you already know that your habit is causing problems between you and what matters, it's only a matter of time until you no longer matter as much to them. The truth hurts and heals. Be honest.

_____

_____

_____

_____

You Matter

Everyone has a purpose whether they recognize it or not. Maybe we confuse how we matter by the scale in which we impact other peoples lives. In reality the scale of our impact is unseen. When we impact our family, our friends and our environment in a positive way, it will ripple outwardly, creating more positivity. Same goes with negativity. Here you can write how you impacted your own world in a positive way. It can be as simple as telling someone else how they matter to you.

_____

_____

_____

_____

YOUR PERSONAL SPACE TO DO AS YOU PLEASE

DATE: _____ **DAY** S M T W T F S

My Why

The best way to stay sober is when you have a strong enough "WHY." Why would you like to stop? Who do you want to stop it for? The WHY can simply be FOR YOURSELF because that will also impact everything and everyone you care about. Take a little time to reflect on your WHY here each day and it will make this journey much easier. It's ok to rewrite the same things here everyday, it's good to remind yourself.

_____

_____

_____

_____

Things that Matter

The fear of losing something important to you can outweigh the gratification of your addiction. Here you can write down the people, places and things that really matter to you. If you already know that your habit is causing problems between you and what matters, it's only a matter of time until you no longer matter as much to them. The truth hurts and heals. Be honest.

_____

_____

_____

_____

You Matter

Everyone has a purpose whether they recognize it or not. Maybe we confuse how we matter by the scale in which we impact other peoples lives. In reality the scale of our impact is unseen. When we impact our family, our friends and our environment in a positive way, it will ripple outwardly, creating more positivity. Same goes with negativity. Here you can write how you impacted your own world in a positive way. It can be as simple as telling someone else how they matter to you.

_____

_____

_____

_____

YOUR PERSONAL SPACE TO DO AS YOU PLEASE

DATE: _____ **DAY** S M T W T F S

My Why

The best way to stay sober is when you have a strong enough "WHY." Why would you like to stop? Who do you want to stop it for? The WHY can simply be FOR YOURSELF because that will also impact everything and everyone you care about. Take a little time to reflect on your WHY here each day and it will make this journey much easier. It's ok to rewrite the same things here everyday, it's good to remind yourself.

_____

_____

_____

_____

Things that Matter

The fear of losing something important to you can outweigh the gratification of your addiction. Here you can write down the people, places and things that really matter to you. If you already know that your habit is causing problems between you and what matters, it's only a matter of time until you no longer matter as much to them. The truth hurts and heals. Be honest.

_____

_____

_____

_____

You Matter

Everyone has a purpose whether they recognize it or not. Maybe we confuse how we matter by the scale in which we impact other peoples lives. In reality the scale of our impact is unseen. When we impact our family, our friends and our environment in a positive way, it will ripple outwardly, creating more positivity. Same goes with negativity. Here you can write how you impacted your own world in a positive way. It can be as simple as telling someone else how they matter to you.

_____

_____

_____

_____

YOUR PERSONAL SPACE TO DO AS YOU PLEASE

My Why

The best way to stay sober is when you have a strong enough "WHY." Why would you like to stop? Who do you want to stop it for? The WHY can simply be FOR YOURSELF because that will also impact everything and everyone you care about. Take a little time to reflect on your WHY here each day and it will make this journey much easier. It's ok to rewrite the same things here everyday, it's good to remind yourself.

_____

_____

_____

_____

Things that Matter

The fear of losing something important to you can outweigh the gratification of your addiction. Here you can write down the people, places and things that really matter to you. If you already know that your habit is causing problems between you and what matters, it's only a matter of time until you no longer matter as much to them. The truth hurts and heals. Be honest.

_____

_____

_____

_____

You Matter

Everyone has a purpose whether they recognize it or not. Maybe we confuse how we matter by the scale in which we impact other peoples lives. In reality the scale of our impact is unseen. When we impact our family, our friends and our environment in a positive way, it will ripple outwardly, creating more positivity. Same goes with negativity. Here you can write how you impacted your own world in a positive way. It can be as simple as telling someone else how they matter to you.

_____

_____

_____

_____

YOUR PERSONAL SPACE TO DO AS YOU PLEASE

DATE: _____   DAY S M T W T F S

My Why

The best way to stay sober is when you have a strong enough "WHY." Why would you like to stop? Who do you want to stop it for? The WHY can simply be FOR YOURSELF because that will also impact everything and everyone you care about. Take a little time to reflect on your WHY here each day and it will make this journey much easier. It's ok to rewrite the same things here everyday, it's good to remind yourself.

_____

_____

_____

_____

Things that Matter

The fear of losing something important to you can outweigh the gratification of your addiction. Here you can write down the people, places and things that really matter to you. If you already know that your habit is causing problems between you and what matters, it's only a matter of time until you no longer matter as much to them. The truth hurts and heals. Be honest.

_____

_____

_____

_____

You Matter

Everyone has a purpose whether they recognize it or not. Maybe we confuse how we matter by the scale in which we impact other peoples lives. In reality the scale of our impact is unseen. When we impact our family, our friends and our environment in a positive way, it will ripple outwardly, creating more positivity. Same goes with negativity. Here you can write how you impacted your own world in a positive way. It can be as simple as telling someone else how they matter to you.

_____

_____

_____

_____

YOUR PERSONAL SPACE TO DO AS YOU PLEASE

DATE: _____   **DAY** S M T W T F S

My Why

The best way to stay sober is when you have a strong enough "WHY." Why would you like to stop? Who do you want to stop it for? The WHY can simply be FOR YOURSELF because that will also impact everything and everyone you care about. Take a little time to reflect on your WHY here each day and it will make this journey much easier. It's ok to rewrite the same things here everyday, it's good to remind yourself.

_____

_____

_____

_____

Things that Matter

The fear of losing something important to you can outweigh the gratification of your addiction. Here you can write down the people, places and things that really matter to you. If you already know that your habit is causing problems between you and what matters, it's only a matter of time until you no longer matter as much to them. The truth hurts and heals. Be honest.

_____

_____

_____

_____

You Matter

Everyone has a purpose whether they recognize it or not. Maybe we confuse how we matter by the scale in which we impact other peoples lives. In reality the scale of our impact is unseen. When we impact our family, our friends and our environment in a positive way, it will ripple outwardly, creating more positivity. Same goes with negativity. Here you can write how you impacted your own world in a positive way. It can be as simple as telling someone else how they matter to you.

_____

_____

_____

_____

My Why

The best way to stay sober is when you have a strong enough "WHY." Why would you like to stop? Who do you want to stop it for? The WHY can simply be FOR YOURSELF because that will also impact everything and everyone you care about. Take a little time to reflect on your WHY here each day and it will make this journey much easier. It's ok to rewrite the same things here everyday, it's good to remind yourself.

_____

_____

_____

Things that Matter

The fear of losing something important to you can outweigh the gratification of your addiction. Here you can write down the people, places and things that really matter to you. If you already know that your habit is causing problems between you and what matters, it's only a matter of time until you no longer matter as much to them. The truth hurts and heals. Be honest.

_____

_____

_____

You Matter

Everyone has a purpose whether they recognize it or not. Maybe we confuse how we matter by the scale in which we impact other peoples lives. In reality the scale of our impact is unseen. When we impact our family, our friends and our environment in a positive way, it will ripple outwardly, creating more positivity. Same goes with negativity. Here you can write how you impacted your own world in a positive way. It can be as simple as telling someone else how they matter to you.

_____

_____

_____

YOUR PERSONAL SPACE TO DO AS YOU PLEASE

DATE: _____ **DAY** S M T W T F S

My Why

The best way to stay sober is when you have a strong enough "WHY." Why would you like to stop? Who do you want to stop it for? The WHY can simply be FOR YOURSELF because that will also impact everything and everyone you care about. Take a little time to reflect on your WHY here each day and it will make this journey much easier. It's ok to rewrite the same things here everyday, it's good to remind yourself.

_____

_____

_____

_____

Things that Matter

The fear of losing something important to you can outweigh the gratification of your addiction. Here you can write down the people, places and things that really matter to you. If you already know that your habit is causing problems between you and what matters, it's only a matter of time until you no longer matter as much to them. The truth hurts and heals. Be honest.

_____

_____

_____

_____

You Matter

Everyone has a purpose whether they recognize it or not. Maybe we confuse how we matter by the scale in which we impact other peoples lives. In reality the scale of our impact is unseen. When we impact our family, our friends and our environment in a positive way, it will ripple outwardly, creating more positivity. Same goes with negativity. Here you can write how you impacted your own world in a positive way. It can be as simple as telling someone else how they matter to you.

_____

_____

_____

_____

YOUR PERSONAL SPACE TO DO AS YOU PLEASE

My Why

The best way to stay sober is when you have a strong enough "WHY." Why would you like to stop? Who do you want to stop it for? The WHY can simply be FOR YOURSELF because that will also impact everything and everyone you care about. Take a little time to reflect on your WHY here each day and it will make this journey much easier. It's ok to rewrite the same things here everyday, it's good to remind yourself.

_____

_____

_____

Things that Matter

The fear of losing something important to you can outweigh the gratification of your addiction. Here you can write down the people, places and things that really matter to you. If you already know that your habit is causing problems between you and what matters, it's only a matter of time until you no longer matter as much to them. The truth hurts and heals. Be honest.

_____

_____

_____

You Matter

Everyone has a purpose whether they recognize it or not. Maybe we confuse how we matter by the scale in which we impact other peoples lives. In reality the scale of our impact is unseen. When we impact our family, our friends and our environment in a positive way, it will ripple outwardly, creating more positivity. Same goes with negativity. Here you can write how you impacted your own world in a positive way. It can be as simple as telling someone else how they matter to you.

_____

_____

_____

YOUR PERSONAL SPACE TO DO AS YOU PLEASE

My Why

The best way to stay sober is when you have a strong enough "WHY." Why would you like to stop? Who do you want to stop it for? The WHY can simply be FOR YOURSELF because that will also impact everything and everyone you care about. Take a little time to reflect on your WHY here each day and it will make this journey much easier. It's ok to rewrite the same things here everyday, it's good to remind yourself.

_____

_____

_____

_____

Things that Matter

The fear of losing something important to you can outweigh the gratification of your addiction. Here you can write down the people, places and things that really matter to you. If you already know that your habit is causing problems between you and what matters, it's only a matter of time until you no longer matter as much to them. The truth hurts and heals. Be honest.

_____

_____

_____

_____

You Matter

Everyone has a purpose whether they recognize it or not. Maybe we confuse how we matter by the scale in which we impact other peoples lives. In reality the scale of our impact is unseen. When we impact our family, our friends and our environment in a positive way, it will ripple outwardly, creating more positivity. Same goes with negativity. Here you can write how you impacted your own world in a positive way. It can be as simple as telling someone else how they matter to you.

_____

_____

_____

_____

YOUR PERSONAL SPACE TO DO AS YOU PLEASE

DATE: _____ DAY S M T W T F S

My Why

The best way to stay sober is when you have a strong enough "WHY." Why would you like to stop? Who do you want to stop it for? The WHY can simply be FOR YOURSELF because that will also impact everything and everyone you care about. Take a little time to reflect on your WHY here each day and it will make this journey much easier. It's ok to rewrite the same things here everyday, it's good to remind yourself.

_____

_____

_____

Things that Matter

The fear of losing something important to you can outweigh the gratification of your addiction. Here you can write down the people, places and things that really matter to you. If you already know that your habit is causing problems between you and what matters, it's only a matter of time until you no longer matter as much to them. The truth hurts and heals. Be honest.

_____

_____

_____

_____

You Matter

Everyone has a purpose whether they recognize it or not. Maybe we confuse how we matter by the scale in which we impact other peoples lives. In reality the scale of our impact is unseen. When we impact our family, our friends and our environment in a positive way, it will ripple outwardly, creating more positivity. Same goes with negativity. Here you can write how you impacted your own world in a positive way. It can be as simple as telling someone else how they matter to you.

_____

_____

_____

_____

YOUR PERSONAL SPACE TO DO AS YOU PLEASE

DATE: _____ **DAY** S M T W T F S

My Why

The best way to stay sober is when you have a strong enough "WHY." Why would you like to stop? Who do you want to stop it for? The WHY can simply be FOR YOURSELF because that will also impact everything and everyone you care about. Take a little time to reflect on your WHY here each day and it will make this journey much easier. It's ok to rewrite the same things here everyday, it's good to remind yourself.

_____

_____

_____

Things that Matter

The fear of losing something important to you can outweigh the gratification of your addiction. Here you can write down the people, places and things that really matter to you. If you already know that your habit is causing problems between you and what matters, it's only a matter of time until you no longer matter as much to them. The truth hurts and heals. Be honest.

_____

_____

_____

You Matter

Everyone has a purpose whether they recognize it or not. Maybe we confuse how we matter by the scale in which we impact other peoples lives. In reality the scale of our impact is unseen. When we impact our family, our friends and our environment in a positive way, it will ripple outwardly, creating more positivity. Same goes with negativity. Here you can write how you impacted your own world in a positive way. It can be as simple as telling someone else how they matter to you.

_____

_____

_____

YOUR PERSONAL SPACE TO DO AS YOU PLEASE

DATE: _____ **DAY** S M T W T F S

My Why

The best way to stay sober is when you have a strong enough "WHY." Why would you like to stop? Who do you want to stop it for? The WHY can simply be FOR YOURSELF because that will also impact everything and everyone you care about. Take a little time to reflect on your WHY here each day and it will make this journey much easier. It's ok to rewrite the same things here everyday, it's good to remind yourself.

_____

_____

_____

Things that Matter

The fear of losing something important to you can outweigh the gratification of your addiction. Here you can write down the people, places and things that really matter to you. If you already know that your habit is causing problems between you and what matters, it's only a matter of time until you no longer matter as much to them. The truth hurts and heals. Be honest.

_____

_____

_____

You Matter

Everyone has a purpose whether they recognize it or not. Maybe we confuse how we matter by the scale in which we impact other peoples lives. In reality the scale of our impact is unseen. When we impact our family, our friends and our environment in a positive way, it will ripple outwardly, creating more positivity. Same goes with negativity. Here you can write how you impacted your own world in a positive way. It can be as simple as telling someone else how they matter to you.

_____

_____

_____

_____

YOUR PERSONAL SPACE TO DO AS YOU PLEASE

DATE: _____   **DAY** S M T W T F S

My Why

The best way to stay sober is when you have a strong enough "WHY." Why would you like to stop? Who do you want to stop it for? The WHY can simply be FOR YOURSELF because that will also impact everything and everyone you care about. Take a little time to reflect on your WHY here each day and it will make this journey much easier. It's ok to rewrite the same things here everyday, it's good to remind yourself.

_____

_____

_____

_____

Things that Matter

The fear of losing something important to you can outweigh the gratification of your addiction. Here you can write down the people, places and things that really matter to you. If you already know that your habit is causing problems between you and what matters, it's only a matter of time until you no longer matter as much to them. The truth hurts and heals. Be honest.

_____

_____

_____

_____

You Matter

Everyone has a purpose whether they recognize it or not. Maybe we confuse how we matter by the scale in which we impact other peoples lives. In reality the scale of our impact is unseen. When we impact our family, our friends and our environment in a positive way, it will ripple outwardly, creating more positivity. Same goes with negativity. Here you can write how you impacted your own world in a positive way. It can be as simple as telling someone else how they matter to you.

_____

_____

_____

_____

YOUR PERSONAL SPACE TO DO AS YOU PLEASE

DATE: _____ **DAY** S M T W T F S

My Why

The best way to stay sober is when you have a strong enough "WHY." Why would you like to stop? Who do you want to stop it for? The WHY can simply be FOR YOURSELF because that will also impact everything and everyone you care about. Take a little time to reflect on your WHY here each day and it will make this journey much easier. It's ok to rewrite the same things here everyday, it's good to remind yourself.

_____

_____

_____

Things that Matter

The fear of losing something important to you can outweigh the gratification of your addiction. Here you can write down the people, places and things that really matter to you. If you already know that your habit is causing problems between you and what matters, it's only a matter of time until you no longer matter as much to them. The truth hurts and heals. Be honest.

_____

_____

_____

You Matter

Everyone has a purpose whether they recognize it or not. Maybe we confuse how we matter by the scale in which we impact other peoples lives. In reality the scale of our impact is unseen. When we impact our family, our friends and our environment in a positive way, it will ripple outwardly, creating more positivity. Same goes with negativity. Here you can write how you impacted your own world in a positive way. It can be as simple as telling someone else how they matter to you.

_____

_____

_____

YOUR PERSONAL SPACE TO DO AS YOU PLEASE

DATE: _____   DAY S M T W T F S

My Why

The best way to stay sober is when you have a strong enough "WHY." Why would you like to stop? Who do you want to stop it for? The WHY can simply be FOR YOURSELF because that will also impact everything and everyone you care about. Take a little time to reflect on your WHY here each day and it will make this journey much easier. It's ok to rewrite the same things here everyday, it's good to remind yourself.

_____

_____

_____

_____

Things that Matter

The fear of losing something important to you can outweigh the gratification of your addiction. Here you can write down the people, places and things that really matter to you. If you already know that your habit is causing problems between you and what matters, it's only a matter of time until you no longer matter as much to them. The truth hurts and heals. Be honest.

_____

_____

_____

_____

You Matter

Everyone has a purpose whether they recognize it or not. Maybe we confuse how we matter by the scale in which we impact other peoples lives. In reality the scale of our impact is unseen. When we impact our family, our friends and our environment in a positive way, it will ripple outwardly, creating more positivity. Same goes with negativity. Here you can write how you impacted your own world in a positive way. It can be as simple as telling someone else how they matter to you.

_____

_____

_____

_____

YOUR PERSONAL SPACE TO DO AS YOU PLEASE

DATE: _____ **DAY** S M T W T F S

My Why

The best way to stay sober is when you have a strong enough "WHY." Why would you like to stop? Who do you want to stop it for? The WHY can simply be FOR YOURSELF because that will also impact everything and everyone you care about. Take a little time to reflect on your WHY here each day and it will make this journey much easier. It's ok to rewrite the same things here everyday, it's good to remind yourself.

_____

_____

_____

_____

Things that Matter

The fear of losing something important to you can outweigh the gratification of your addiction. Here you can write down the people, places and things that really matter to you. If you already know that your habit is causing problems between you and what matters, it's only a matter of time until you no longer matter as much to them. The truth hurts and heals. Be honest.

_____

_____

_____

_____

You Matter

Everyone has a purpose whether they recognize it or not. Maybe we confuse how we matter by the scale in which we impact other peoples lives. In reality the scale of our impact is unseen. When we impact our family, our friends and our environment in a positive way, it will ripple outwardly, creating more positivity. Same goes with negativity. Here you can write how you impacted your own world in a positive way. It can be as simple as telling someone else how they matter to you.

_____

_____

_____

_____

YOUR PERSONAL SPACE TO DO AS YOU PLEASE

DATE: _____   **DAY** S M T W T F S

My Why

The best way to stay sober is when you have a strong enough "WHY." Why would you like to stop? Who do you want to stop it for? The WHY can simply be FOR YOURSELF because that will also impact everything and everyone you care about. Take a little time to reflect on your WHY here each day and it will make this journey much easier. It's ok to rewrite the same things here everyday, it's good to remind yourself.

_____

_____

_____

Things that Matter

The fear of losing something important to you can outweigh the gratification of your addiction. Here you can write down the people, places and things that really matter to you. If you already know that your habit is causing problems between you and what matters, it's only a matter of time until you no longer matter as much to them. The truth hurts and heals. Be honest.

_____

_____

_____

You Matter

Everyone has a purpose whether they recognize it or not. Maybe we confuse how we matter by the scale in which we impact other peoples lives. In reality the scale of our impact is unseen. When we impact our family, our friends and our environment in a positive way, it will ripple outwardly, creating more positivity. Same goes with negativity. Here you can write how you impacted your own world in a positive way. It can be as simple as telling someone else how they matter to you.

_____

_____

_____

YOUR PERSONAL SPACE TO DO AS YOU PLEASE

DATE: _____

My Why

The best way to stay sober is when you have a strong enough "WHY." Why would you like to stop? Who do you want to stop it for? The WHY can simply be FOR YOURSELF because that will also impact everything and everyone you care about. Take a little time to reflect on your WHY here each day and it will make this journey much easier. It's ok to rewrite the same things here everyday, it's good to remind yourself.

_____

_____

_____

_____

Things that Matter

The fear of losing something important to you can outweigh the gratification of your addiction. Here you can write down the people, places and things that really matter to you. If you already know that your habit is causing problems between you and what matters, it's only a matter of time until you no longer matter as much to them. The truth hurts and heals. Be honest.

_____

_____

_____

_____

You Matter

Everyone has a purpose whether they recognize it or not. Maybe we confuse how we matter by the scale in which we impact other peoples lives. In reality the scale of our impact is unseen. When we impact our family, our friends and our environment in a positive way, it will ripple outwardly, creating more positivity. Same goes with negativity. Here you can write how you impacted your own world in a positive way. It can be as simple as telling someone else how they matter to you.

_____

_____

_____

_____

YOUR PERSONAL SPACE TO DO AS YOU PLEASE

My Why

The best way to stay sober is when you have a strong enough "WHY." Why would you like to stop? Who do you want to stop it for? The WHY can simply be FOR YOURSELF because that will also impact everything and everyone you care about. Take a little time to reflect on your WHY here each day and it will make this journey much easier. It's ok to rewrite the same things here everyday, it's good to remind yourself.

_____

_____

_____

_____

Things that Matter

The fear of losing something important to you can outweigh the gratification of your addiction. Here you can write down the people, places and things that really matter to you. If you already know that your habit is causing problems between you and what matters, it's only a matter of time until you no longer matter as much to them. The truth hurts and heals. Be honest.

_____

_____

_____

_____

You Matter

Everyone has a purpose whether they recognize it or not. Maybe we confuse how we matter by the scale in which we impact other peoples lives. In reality the scale of our impact is unseen. When we impact our family, our friends and our environment in a positive way, it will ripple outwardly, creating more positivity. Same goes with negativity. Here you can write how you impacted your own world in a positive way. It can be as simple as telling someone else how they matter to you.

_____

_____

_____

_____

YOUR PERSONAL SPACE TO DO AS YOU PLEASE

DATE: _____ **DAY** S M T W T F S

My Why

The best way to stay sober is when you have a strong enough "WHY." Why would you like to stop? Who do you want to stop it for? The WHY can simply be FOR YOURSELF because that will also impact everything and everyone you care about. Take a little time to reflect on your WHY here each day and it will make this journey much easier. It's ok to rewrite the same things here everyday, it's good to remind yourself.

_____

_____

_____

_____

Things that Matter

The fear of losing something important to you can outweigh the gratification of your addiction. Here you can write down the people, places and things that really matter to you. If you already know that your habit is causing problems between you and what matters, it's only a matter of time until you no longer matter as much to them. The truth hurts and heals. Be honest.

_____

_____

_____

_____

You Matter

Everyone has a purpose whether they recognize it or not. Maybe we confuse how we matter by the scale in which we impact other peoples lives. In reality the scale of our impact is unseen. When we impact our family, our friends and our environment in a positive way, it will ripple outwardly, creating more positivity. Same goes with negativity. Here you can write how you impacted your own world in a positive way. It can be as simple as telling someone else how they matter to you.

_____

_____

_____

_____

YOUR PERSONAL SPACE TO DO AS YOU PLEASE

DATE: _____   **DAY S M T W T F S**

My Why

The best way to stay sober is when you have a strong enough "WHY." Why would you like to stop? Who do you want to stop it for? The WHY can simply be FOR YOURSELF because that will also impact everything and everyone you care about. Take a little time to reflect on your WHY here each day and it will make this journey much easier. It's ok to rewrite the same things here everyday, it's good to remind yourself.

_____

_____

_____

_____

Things that Matter

The fear of losing something important to you can outweigh the gratification of your addiction. Here you can write down the people, places and things that really matter to you. If you already know that your habit is causing problems between you and what matters, it's only a matter of time until you no longer matter as much to them. The truth hurts and heals. Be honest.

_____

_____

_____

_____

You Matter

Everyone has a purpose whether they recognize it or not. Maybe we confuse how we matter by the scale in which we impact other peoples lives. In reality the scale of our impact is unseen. When we impact our family, our friends and our environment in a positive way, it will ripple outwardly, creating more positivity. Same goes with negativity. Here you can write how you impacted your own world in a positive way. It can be as simple as telling someone else how they matter to you.

_____

_____

_____

_____

YOUR PERSONAL SPACE TO DO AS YOU PLEASE

DATE: _____ **DAY** S M T W T F S

My Why

The best way to stay sober is when you have a strong enough "WHY." Why would you like to stop? Who do you want to stop it for? The WHY can simply be FOR YOURSELF because that will also impact everything and everyone you care about. Take a little time to reflect on your WHY here each day and it will make this journey much easier. It's ok to rewrite the same things here everyday, it's good to remind yourself.

_____

_____

_____

_____

Things that Matter

The fear of losing something important to you can outweigh the gratification of your addiction. Here you can write down the people, places and things that really matter to you. If you already know that your habit is causing problems between you and what matters, it's only a matter of time until you no longer matter as much to them. The truth hurts and heals. Be honest.

_____

_____

_____

_____

You Matter

Everyone has a purpose whether they recognize it or not. Maybe we confuse how we matter by the scale in which we impact other peoples lives. In reality the scale of our impact is unseen. When we impact our family, our friends and our environment in a positive way, it will ripple outwardly, creating more positivity. Same goes with negativity. Here you can write how you impacted your own world in a positive way. It can be as simple as telling someone else how they matter to you.

_____

_____

_____

_____

YOUR PERSONAL SPACE TO DO AS YOU PLEASE

DATE: _____ **DAY** S M T W T F S

My Why

The best way to stay sober is when you have a strong enough "WHY." Why would you like to stop? Who do you want to stop it for? The WHY can simply be FOR YOURSELF because that will also impact everything and everyone you care about. Take a little time to reflect on your WHY here each day and it will make this journey much easier. It's ok to rewrite the same things here everyday, it's good to remind yourself.

_____

_____

_____

_____

Things that Matter

The fear of losing something important to you can outweigh the gratification of your addiction. Here you can write down the people, places and things that really matter to you. If you already know that your habit is causing problems between you and what matters, it's only a matter of time until you no longer matter as much to them. The truth hurts and heals. Be honest.

_____

_____

_____

_____

You Matter

Everyone has a purpose whether they recognize it or not. Maybe we confuse how we matter by the scale in which we impact other peoples lives. In reality the scale of our impact is unseen. When we impact our family, our friends and our environment in a positive way, it will ripple outwardly, creating more positivity. Same goes with negativity. Here you can write how you impacted your own world in a positive way. It can be as simple as telling someone else how they matter to you.

_____

_____

_____

_____

YOUR PERSONAL SPACE TO DO AS YOU PLEASE

My Why

The best way to stay sober is when you have a strong enough "WHY." Why would you like to stop? Who do you want to stop it for? The WHY can simply be FOR YOURSELF because that will also impact everything and everyone you care about. Take a little time to reflect on your WHY here each day and it will make this journey much easier. It's ok to rewrite the same things here everyday, it's good to remind yourself.

_____

_____

_____

Things that Matter

The fear of losing something important to you can outweigh the gratification of your addiction. Here you can write down the people, places and things that really matter to you. If you already know that your habit is causing problems between you and what matters, it's only a matter of time until you no longer matter as much to them. The truth hurts and heals. Be honest.

_____

_____

_____

You Matter

Everyone has a purpose whether they recognize it or not. Maybe we confuse how we matter by the scale in which we impact other peoples lives. In reality the scale of our impact is unseen. When we impact our family, our friends and our environment in a positive way, it will ripple outwardly, creating more positivity. Same goes with negativity. Here you can write how you impacted your own world in a positive way. It can be as simple as telling someone else how they matter to you.

_____

_____

_____

YOUR PERSONAL SPACE TO DO AS YOU PLEASE

My Why

The best way to stay sober is when you have a strong enough "WHY." Why would you like to stop? Who do you want to stop it for? The WHY can simply be FOR YOURSELF because that will also impact everything and everyone you care about. Take a little time to reflect on your WHY here each day and it will make this journey much easier. It's ok to rewrite the same things here everyday, it's good to remind yourself.

_____

_____

_____

_____

Things that Matter

The fear of losing something important to you can outweigh the gratification of your addiction. Here you can write down the people, places and things that really matter to you. If you already know that your habit is causing problems between you and what matters, it's only a matter of time until you no longer matter as much to them. The truth hurts and heals. Be honest.

_____

_____

_____

_____

You Matter

Everyone has a purpose whether they recognize it or not. Maybe we confuse how we matter by the scale in which we impact other peoples lives. In reality the scale of our impact is unseen. When we impact our family, our friends and our environment in a positive way, it will ripple outwardly, creating more positivity. Same goes with negativity. Here you can write how you impacted your own world in a positive way. It can be as simple as telling someone else how they matter to you.

_____

_____

_____

_____

YOUR PERSONAL SPACE TO DO AS YOU PLEASE

DATE: _____ **DAY** S M T W T F S

My Why

The best way to stay sober is when you have a strong enough "WHY." Why would you like to stop? Who do you want to stop it for? The WHY can simply be FOR YOURSELF because that will also impact everything and everyone you care about. Take a little time to reflect on your WHY here each day and it will make this journey much easier. It's ok to rewrite the same things here everyday, it's good to remind yourself.

_____

_____

_____

Things that Matter

The fear of losing something important to you can outweigh the gratification of your addiction. Here you can write down the people, places and things that really matter to you. If you already know that your habit is causing problems between you and what matters, it's only a matter of time until you no longer matter as much to them. The truth hurts and heals. Be honest.

_____

_____

_____

You Matter

Everyone has a purpose whether they recognize it or not. Maybe we confuse how we matter by the scale in which we impact other peoples lives. In reality the scale of our impact is unseen. When we impact our family, our friends and our environment in a positive way, it will ripple outwardly, creating more positivity. Same goes with negativity. Here you can write how you impacted your own world in a positive way. It can be as simple as telling someone else how they matter to you.

_____

_____

_____

YOUR PERSONAL SPACE TO DO AS YOU PLEASE

DATE: _____ **DAY** S M T W T F S

My Why

The best way to stay sober is when you have a strong enough "WHY." Why would you like to stop? Who do you want to stop it for? The WHY can simply be FOR YOURSELF because that will also impact everything and everyone you care about. Take a little time to reflect on your WHY here each day and it will make this journey much easier. It's ok to rewrite the same things here everyday, it's good to remind yourself.

_____

_____

_____

_____

Things that Matter

The fear of losing something important to you can outweigh the gratification of your addiction. Here you can write down the people, places and things that really matter to you. If you already know that your habit is causing problems between you and what matters, it's only a matter of time until you no longer matter as much to them. The truth hurts and heals. Be honest.

_____

_____

_____

_____

You Matter

Everyone has a purpose whether they recognize it or not. Maybe we confuse how we matter by the scale in which we impact other peoples lives. In reality the scale of our impact is unseen. When we impact our family, our friends and our environment in a positive way, it will ripple outwardly, creating more positivity. Same goes with negativity. Here you can write how you impacted your own world in a positive way. It can be as simple as telling someone else how they matter to you.

_____

_____

_____

_____

YOUR PERSONAL SPACE TO DO AS YOU PLEASE

DATE: _____ **DAY** S M T W T F S

My Why

The best way to stay sober is when you have a strong enough "WHY." Why would you like to stop? Who do you want to stop it for? The WHY can simply be FOR YOURSELF because that will also impact everything and everyone you care about. Take a little time to reflect on your WHY here each day and it will make this journey much easier. It's ok to rewrite the same things here everyday, it's good to remind yourself.

_____

_____

_____

_____

Things that Matter

The fear of losing something important to you can outweigh the gratification of your addiction. Here you can write down the people, places and things that really matter to you. If you already know that your habit is causing problems between you and what matters, it's only a matter of time until you no longer matter as much to them. The truth hurts and heals. Be honest.

_____

_____

_____

_____

You Matter

Everyone has a purpose whether they recognize it or not. Maybe we confuse how we matter by the scale in which we impact other peoples lives. In reality the scale of our impact is unseen. When we impact our family, our friends and our environment in a positive way, it will ripple outwardly, creating more positivity. Same goes with negativity. Here you can write how you impacted your own world in a positive way. It can be as simple as telling someone else how they matter to you.

_____

_____

_____

_____

YOUR PERSONAL SPACE TO DO AS YOU PLEASE

DATE: _____   **DAY** S M T W T F S

My Why

The best way to stay sober is when you have a strong enough "WHY." Why would you like to stop? Who do you want to stop it for? The WHY can simply be FOR YOURSELF because that will also impact everything and everyone you care about. Take a little time to reflect on your WHY here each day and it will make this journey much easier. It's ok to rewrite the same things here everyday, it's good to remind yourself.

_____

_____

_____

Things that Matter

The fear of losing something important to you can outweigh the gratification of your addiction. Here you can write down the people, places and things that really matter to you. If you already know that your habit is causing problems between you and what matters, it's only a matter of time until you no longer matter as much to them. The truth hurts and heals. Be honest.

_____

_____

_____

You Matter

Everyone has a purpose whether they recognize it or not. Maybe we confuse how we matter by the scale in which we impact other peoples lives. In reality the scale of our impact is unseen. When we impact our family, our friends and our environment in a positive way, it will ripple outwardly, creating more positivity. Same goes with negativity. Here you can write how you impacted your own world in a positive way. It can be as simple as telling someone else how they matter to you.

_____

_____

_____

YOUR PERSONAL SPACE TO DO AS YOU PLEASE

My Why

The best way to stay sober is when you have a strong enough "WHY." Why would you like to stop? Who do you want to stop it for? The WHY can simply be FOR YOURSELF because that will also impact everything and everyone you care about. Take a little time to reflect on your WHY here each day and it will make this journey much easier. It's ok to rewrite the same things here everyday, it's good to remind yourself.

_____

_____

_____

Things that Matter

The fear of losing something important to you can outweigh the gratification of your addiction. Here you can write down the people, places and things that really matter to you. If you already know that your habit is causing problems between you and what matters, it's only a matter of time until you no longer matter as much to them. The truth hurts and heals. Be honest.

_____

_____

_____

You Matter

Everyone has a purpose whether they recognize it or not. Maybe we confuse how we matter by the scale in which we impact other peoples lives. In reality the scale of our impact is unseen. When we impact our family, our friends and our environment in a positive way, it will ripple outwardly, creating more positivity. Same goes with negativity. Here you can write how you impacted your own world in a positive way. It can be as simple as telling someone else how they matter to you.

_____

_____

_____

YOUR PERSONAL SPACE TO DO AS YOU PLEASE

DATE: _____   DAY S M T W T F S

My Why

The best way to stay sober is when you have a strong enough "WHY." Why would you like to stop? Who do you want to stop it for? The WHY can simply be FOR YOURSELF because that will also impact everything and everyone you care about. Take a little time to reflect on your WHY here each day and it will make this journey much easier. It's ok to rewrite the same things here everyday, it's good to remind yourself.

_____

_____

_____

Things that Matter

The fear of losing something important to you can outweigh the gratification of your addiction. Here you can write down the people, places and things that really matter to you. If you already know that your habit is causing problems between you and what matters, it's only a matter of time until you no longer matter as much to them. The truth hurts and heals. Be honest.

_____

_____

_____

You Matter

Everyone has a purpose whether they recognize it or not. Maybe we confuse how we matter by the scale in which we impact other peoples lives. In reality the scale of our impact is unseen. When we impact our family, our friends and our environment in a positive way, it will ripple outwardly, creating more positivity. Same goes with negativity. Here you can write how you impacted your own world in a positive way. It can be as simple as telling someone else how they matter to you.

_____

_____

_____